Refuel Sis

You Have Work To Do

Renee Goings Richardson

Copyright © 2023 Renee Goings Richardson

All rights reserved.

ISBN:

All scriptures are referenced from the
King James Version of the Holy Bible

Dedication

To my mom:

The woman that I am today is a direct reflection of who you are. Your endless example of integrity causes me to strive to live a life that is holy and pleasing to God. I am encouraged by you daily. May God grant me the wisdom to continue to follow in your footsteps.

Contents

	Introduction	i
1	So, Who Are You?	1
2	How Did I Get Here?	7
3	Is This Really Happening?	13
4	Um, Who Are You Talking To?	21
5	Was That Shade?	25
6	But, Why?	33
7	Who Told You That?	37

Introduction

She followed behind the bright red PT Cruiser carefully observing the passing cars. The highway was congested, but traffic was steady. After working on her feet for several hours, thoughts of home comforted her. Although grateful for employment, she took no joy in her current job. How could such a happy place for others cause misery to her? Suddenly, the red Cruiser slammed on brakes. Frightened by what had happened, she did the same and came to an abrupt stop.

She felt a sigh of relief knowing she had not rear-ended the vehicle. However, she grew fearful as the white pickup truck behind her quickly approached. "Please stop, please stop!" she screamed. Within seconds her car spun around in circles uncontrollably. She grasped the steering wheel tighter and tighter. She felt the car being hit with each spin. Peering out the driver's window, she could see the trailer that was no longer attached to the white pickup truck coming her way. "JESUS, JESUS, JESUS!" she cried, as her car perched on the side of the bridge.

She saw the brown murky water from the river sitting below her. Terrified that her car would tilt over, she wailed in fear. Within seconds she felt her car being hit again. This time she closed her eyes and braced herself for what would happen next. Once the spinning stopped, she opened her eyes and realized she was still on the bridge. Anxious and thankful, she looked to the right side of her car. A man in a white t-shirt was talking to her through her window. "Are you ok?" he asked.

"Yes. My door handle is broken. I can't get out. Please unlock the door for me," she said. With apprehension, she watched as he reached his hand through the broken glass and unlocked the doors.

Pushing the airbag away from her face and then forcing the door open, she exited the car. Happy to be alive, she paced the ground to gather her thoughts. "Do you have insurance?" an older gentleman asked as he and his wife approached.

Realizing they were the drivers of the red PT Cruiser, she chuckled. "Yes, I do and I'm fine. Thanks for asking," she responded.

Almost immediately, another couple approached. "Sweetheart, are you ok? You're bleeding. Come sit down." the wife insisted.

"Yes ma'am. I'm fine. I don't know where my phone is though. Do you have one I can use to call my parents," she questioned?

"Absolutely," she said, and gave the young lady her phone. After speaking to her parents and assuring them she was ok, she heard the sounds of multiple sirens. Paramedics went rushing over to her vehicle, only to find it empty. Confused, they began to look around. "She's over here," the helpful couple exclaimed. They wheeled a stretcher her way, insisting she sit down.

Convinced she was fine, she reluctantly sat down. They pushed her into the ambulance and began to ask her a series of questions. Confident they were overreacting, she attempted to answer their questions and once again assure them of her well-being.

"Ma'am, can you move your arm?" the paramedic asked.

"Huh," she said.

"Ma'am, your arm is swollen and bleeding. You have kept it bent and held close to your body. Also, your leg is bleeding. Do you mind if we examine you? We will need to cut your pants to take a further look," stated the EMT.

Her adrenaline was pumping. She hadn't noticed the blood or felt any pain. Now rethinking the accident, she asks the paramedic, "Is it that bad?"

With a concerned look, the paramedic responds and

says, "Based on the look of your car, you're lucky to be alive. You definitely need to be examined."

If you have ever been in an automobile accident, you may have heard screeching brakes, clanking metal or even screams. They are sounds that are associated with oncoming calamity. Wouldn't it be great to be able to hear screeching brakes to serve as a warning about life's obstacles? Think of all the misfortunes you could have avoided if you knew about them in advance. Most individuals would make detours and choose different routes.

Unfortunately, life does not work that way. God allows us to experience unavoidable hardships to build our character and teach us how to press our way through situations. During those obstacles, we must choose the best solution for our problem. The merry-go-round of life can resemble the above accident. Problems can continue to hit you and feel as if they will never stop. Please be assured in knowing that God has equipped you to handle whatever has happened, is happening, or is going to happen. He is the one who gives us the fuel we need to succeed. So, gas up! Dust off that bible. Now open it and read it attentively! Spend time in prayer! There is work for you to do and YOU   CAN   DO   THIS

Chapter One

SO, WHO ARE YOU?

She gasps for air and rubs her eyes. The faint screeching sound grows louder as she fumbles to locate her phone. She exhales and breathes heavily. It's 6:30 a.m. "Get up, get up," she whispers to herself. "Fifteen more minutes won't hurt," she says then yawns and turns over. Her breathing slows and she closes her eyes. A feeling of comfort and relief gently hugs her body. Her mind drifts and she imagines herself lying in a field of billowy softness.

Suddenly her place of peace is disrupted with familiar reminders of numerous responsibilities. Her ears ring and her heart skips a beat as her snoozed alarm startles her. "Ok, it's 6:45. You need to get up," she utters to herself but remains still. "God, please help me," she murmurs and grabs her phone. Its shrill sounds irritate her. She presses snooze for the last time.

A flood of "to-dos" engulfs her mind. She dreads getting up, but now they are louder than her blaring alarm clock. Much like a string puppet, she lifts her head followed by her limbs, and allows her feet to touch the floor. "I'm up," she says. "I'm up." She stumbles to the bathroom, empties her bladder, and turns on the shower while mentally planning her day. The warm water mists her face and body, but doesn't seem to truly awaken her.

While brushing her teeth, she wonders where her multivitamins are. T-shirts and leggings are now the staple of her daily attire. She selects black leggings and a black tee-shirt. After getting dressed, she examines the house. "Today's a new day," she whispers. She then walks through the house and attempts to collect dirty linen, pick up toys, sweep floors, wipe down counters, wash linen, fold linen and cook breakfast before the children awake. It is 7:15 a.m. and she is already tired.

Have you experienced this level of exhaustion? I am persuaded many women are not operating at their full potential. They are simply existing. Their daily routine is habitual and predictable. They do not have to prep or study for their life roles. They operate off fumes while attending to the needs of their family and simultaneously neglecting their well-being. They are excellent actors. They know how to play cook, maid, doctor, bus driver, teacher, lover, and friend with a loving smile.

Meanwhile, they lack physical and mental energy.

Their tanks are on low and have been for some time. They are numb in many areas of their life. They focus all of their attention toward others and save little for themselves. The truth is, your family benefits most from the best version of you.

SO, WHO ARE YOU?

1. **You are a beautifully crafted masterpiece.**

   Psalms 139:14 says, "I will praise thee; for I am

   fearfully and wonderfully made: marvellous are thy works; and that my soul knoweth right well."

   The word fearfully means to revere, to stand in awe of, and to cause astonishment. Wonderfully means to be distinct, marked out, separated, and distinguished. Do you know you are a woman of distinction? When God made you, He took a step back and said, "Wow!"

2. **You are so special that He saved you for last.**

   Genesis 2:21-22 says, "And the Lord God caused a deep sleep to fall upon Adam, and he slept: and he took one of his ribs, and closed up the flesh instead thereof; And the rib, which the Lord God had taken from man, made he a woman, and brought her unto the man."

After forming everything else, He took His time and created you. He did not want distractions. He did not want interruptions. He made Adam go to bed. Then, He created woman. There is a saying that says, "Save the best for last." Let me toot your horn. You were created last. Sis, you are the best!

3. You are royalty.

I Peter 2:9 says, "But ye are a chosen generation, a royal priesthood, an holy nation, a peculiar people; that ye should shew forth the praises of him who hath called you out of darkness into his marvellous light:"

Go ahead and fix your crown. You are chosen for whatever the task is that seems unconquerable. You are the perfect fit. Nobody else can be that mother, sister, wife, lover, friend, co-worker, caretaker, teacher, employee, boss, banker, beautician (and all the other titles you have) but YOU. From now on, address yourself with honor. Look in the mirror and speak to that image that stares back. Declare your place of authority and walk in it. Give adoration to God for allowing you to be in the position that you are in. Every time you make bold affirmations over yourself, you unlock the chains of self-pity.

PRAYER

Father, your word declares that I am fearfully and wonderfully made. I believe that I am special in your sight. My uniqueness is so important that you decided to create me last. I have been called out especially by you to shine. Allow the light of your love to glow through me and ignite a fire for you in others. Help me to remember who I am and forgive me for not believing what your word says about me. I decree and declare that I will strive to live a life pleasing to you. Amen.

Chapter Two

HOW DID I GET HERE?

She stood there peering through the glass restraints. "Green, brown, green," she thought. She was motionless but felt as if she were on an emotional carousel. The urge to wail was raging inside her much like the wailing coming from the infant she heard in the distant background. Her shirt was wet. Her breasts were swollen and sore. She felt heavy and restrained. Nothing made sense in her head. "Is that a baby," she asked herself. "Ok, I see green, brown, green," she thought. There was a muffled noise inside her head that grew louder. "Am I standing up? Why am I sinking?" she thought. The crying intensified and nothing made sense to her. "Trees. Those are trees," she thought, as she continued to glare puzzlingly through the window.

She wanted to escape the noises. She gasped as the pain in her stomach increased. She ached. Moving slowly away from the window, she felt compelled to follow the whimpering sound. She moved closer to the sobbing. Not only was it a baby, it was her baby. "Oh my God. What am I supposed to do," she sighed. She envisioned herself comforting the child, but there was a disconnect. She sat on the couch next to the bassinet. Breathing slowly, she whispered under breath and said, "How did I get here?"

She cautiously reached into the bassinet and cradled the whimpering infant. Gently positioning the child, she proceeded to breastfeed. The initial latch of the newborn's mouth onto her nipple felt like a strong pinch. It hurt, but she continued to hold and nurse her little one. Her other breast began to leak. She reached for the suction cup and placed it onto her other breast. The growls of her stomach intensified, and she realized she had not eaten. The baby finished nursing and almost immediately burped when sat upright. The mom winced, as a result of the pain from her incision, while attempting to reposition herself. After a diaper change, the infant went back to sleep and was placed back in the bassinet.

She stared at the television. It was blank, like her. The power was not on and neither was hers. The location of the remote control was irrelevant. She lacked the strength and desire to search for it. So, she sat and looked at the black screen. Without reason, tears fell from her eyes. She wept in silence. Her head spun and she felt dizzy, even her thoughts were hazy.

Slowly and carefully, she maneuvered her body in

order to stand up. She made her way into the kitchen. After locating the storage bags for the remaining breast milk, she took a few sips of water. Her throat was dry, really dry. After eating the granola bar, she labeled the breast milk and placed it in the freezer. She felt slightly better.

The sad reality of motherhood is that many women experience postpartum following the birth of their child. Life can mirror many of the phases a woman experiences before, during, and after pregnancy. The joys of having a precious little one can be overshadowed by feelings of despair. Without realizing what has happened, many mothers find themselves battling after giving birth.

If you have ever witnessed your dreams be fulfilled, your experience may have mimicked that of a postpartum mother. Disclaimer: They are absolutely NOT the same. However, just like the mother needs to care for the baby, the dreamer will have to constantly provide care for their fulfilled aspirations. The excitement surrounding the ambitions being brought to life and then the struggle to maintain it can be overwhelming. All goals have a pregnancy phase, a birthing phase, and also an afterbirth process. Depression can easily set in during any of the phases. You may also find yourself sharing the same question as the mother.

HOW DID I GET HERE?

When attacking depression, these are a few of the proclamations to remember.

1. **You are not alone.**

    Isaiah 41:10 says, "Fear thou not; for I am with thee: be not dismayed; for I am thy God: I will strengthen thee; yea, I will help thee; yea, I will uphold thee with the right hand of my righteousness."

Depression almost works like an eraser. It has a way of deleting certain things. You can sit in a room with others and not see, hear, or feel anyone. Sometimes, those very people have been sent by God to help you. Don't push your help away.

2. **These feelings are temporary. This too shall pass.**

    Ecclesiastes 3:1 says, "To every thing there is a season, and a time to every purpose under the heaven:"

If you can choose to think differently, your current feelings will one day be your past feelings. The key is to remember it is just a season. One day you will be able to look back, know it happened and be unbothered.

3. **You do not have to feed the spirit of depression. Starve it. Speak life. Give it a change of address.**

   I Samuel 3:6 says, "And David was greatly distressed; for the people spake of stoning him, because the soul of all the people was grieved, every man for his sons and for his daughters: but David encouraged himself in the LORD his God."

After experiencing a huge loss, David faced depression. Individuals that once admired him, now loathed him. Rather than sulk in his sadness, he found hope. He spoke life to himself. You too, must choose to speak to yourself and your situation. Anything that is fed will grow. If you feed your mind hope, you will experience healing. If you feed your depressive state, it will expand. Do not allow it to have a permanent address in your life. Go ahead and give it the change of address form. Tell depression it is no longer welcome in your life.

4. **Seek help.**

   Matthew 7:7 says, "Ask, and it shall be given you; seek, and ye shall find; knock, and it shall be opened unto you:"

While we acknowledge God to be our healer, there are instances where you may need to seek medical attention. I am a firm believer that God can work through medical professionals to help individuals. Chemical imbalances require medical attention. Take your medicine as you continue to pray for your healing.

PRAYER

Lord, help me to overcome these feelings that have been attacking my mind. Strengthen me. Speak to me. Live in me. I rebuke the feelings of loneliness. I AM NOT ALONE. I know you are with me. I pray against the spirit of stagnation. Break every chain that has held my mind in captivity. Release me from the clutches of depression and any other sin that has attached itself to me. Lead me to the right individuals that can help me. Continue to cover me with your love and protection. Amen.

Chapter Three

IS THIS REALLY HAPPENING?

During the middle of a chaotic work day, she leaves the office to perform a few of her managerial duties. Deposits must be made and mail must go out. She cranks her car in hopes of driving to the bank and post office. Her gas needle is resting on the left side of E. She sighs and says, "Oh Lord, I forgot to get gas yesterday." Unfortunately, there is a temporary gas shortage. Therefore, the gas station is packed and tensions are high, as people wait in line. She finally pulls up to a pump and breathes deeply. There is a sign instructing her to pay inside. Paying at the pump is her preferred method. Going inside the store takes much more time. After all, time is of the essence.

She shuts the engine off, grabs her keys and purse, then musters up a smile. "Thank you," she says to the gentleman holding the door. Several patrons stood in front of her waiting to pay for their gas. A woman purchasing cigarettes and lottery tickets tested the patience of everyone in the line, along with the cashier. "Please hurry up," she thought. Heavy exhalations echoed from behind her. Apparently, she wasn't the only one anticipating a quicker process. After paying for her gas, she is elated to exit the store.

Upon approaching her car, she notices her gas tank is on the opposite side of the vehicle. Chuckling to herself, she moves her vehicle forward to turn it around. She attempts to back up, but her vehicle stalls and then completely stops. Another vehicle is attempting to park beside her prepaid pump. She then realizes her car is completely out of fuel. "Is this really happening," she gripes. Without the slightest idea of how she would handle the situation, she gets out of her vehicle. She instructs the ambitious driver that payment has been made for the gas at that pump. An older gentleman with a pick-up truck notices her dilemma. She is embarrassed. Somehow, he knows exactly what has happened and has a gas can on the back of his truck. He puts some gas in her tank and instructs her to turn it on. Her vehicle cranks without hesitation. She thanks him and attempts to re-pay him for his fuel. He refuses the money and tells her she is welcome. To save herself from further embarrassment, she looks around for familiar faces, quickly pumps her gas and then leaves.

The fact that she was so close to refueling her vehicle and still ran out of gas at the pump is almost unbelievable. I believe many Christians mimic her behavior in their walk with God. We live our lives on E, barely refueling our spirit man. We attend church regularly. We have a relationship with Christ and live our lives according to the doctrine of Christ, but we're operating on fumes. We're actually spiritually malnourished. Ask yourself if your spirit man mimics the behavior of this young lady.

- **She knew her fuel level was low.**

  Do you refuel your spirit man daily or do you ride around until your tank gets to E?

- **She was in the right place to refuel her vehicle but she was turned in the wrong direction.**

  Do you find yourself distracted during personal prayer time or service? Do you allow your mind to roam during the preached word? If you're in service, does your attention shift to the person sitting in front of you? Do you follow the movement of the ushers? Do you play with your phone or electronic device while the message is being delivered? If you're viewing the message from home, is your heart positioned to receive God's word or are you busy making dinner?

- **She repositions her vehicle to get to the gas pump, but she only has fumes left.** Do you attempt to reposition your mind during service, but realize you are further away than you thought?
- **A gentleman comes to help her. He has what she needs and did not want anything in return.** Have you received a random call or text message from someone that offered words of encouragement?

IS THIS REALLY HAPPENING?

If you are currently stalling, **REFUEL**! Here's how:

1. **Renew your mind.**

    Romans 12:2 says, "And be not conformed to this world: but be ye transformed by the renewing of your mind, that ye may prove what is that good, and acceptable, and perfect, will of God."

The Strongs Concordance references the word "renewing"

as a complete change for the better. A renewed mind equals a revamped way of thinking. If you think differently, you will act differently.

2. Eliminate any carnal habits that draw you away from Christ.

*2 Corinthians 5:17 says, Therefore if any man be in Christ, he is a **new creature**: old things are passed away; behold, all things are become **new**.*

It is absolutely necessary to change any practices that do not honor God. When changes are implemented, it may take time for those decisions to become natural to you. As you continue to practice them, you will become familiar with them. Things that were hinderances will not bother you the way they use to. However, it is a continual effort. You must stand firm in your decision to remove yourself from the things of old.

3. Form and maintain healthy God-given relationships.

1 Corinthians 15:33 says, "Be not deceived: evil communications corrupt good manners."

The company you keep matters. Who you hang around influences your thoughts and impacts your character. If you associate with thieves, you will be influenced by the thieves. I have witnessed individuals make light of wrong because their company had desensitized their thinking. When the truth becomes optional, you have a problem. This does not mean you cannot speak to individuals that do not share your beliefs. We must witness to the lost. Keep in mind, there will always be an influencer. Sometimes, it may NOT be you.

4. **Usher the presence of the Lord into your life daily through prayer.**

   Psalm 27:4 says, "One thing have I desired of the LORD, that will I seek after; that I may dwell in the house of the LORD all the days of my life, to behold the beauty of the LORD, and to enquire in his temple.

When refueling your spirit, being in the presence of the Lord must become habitual. Your desperation to be near the Father will impact every facet of your life. His existence will become as prevalent as the air you breathe. Your daily prayer life allows you to draw closer to God. As you welcome him, he can reside within you.

5. **Exercise your faith. Speak it. Believe it.**

   2 Corinthians 5:7 says, "For we walk by faith, not by sight:"

In the natural, physical training requires commitment and dedication. To achieve your desired level of fitness, you must exert a continual effort. Your results aren't always visible. Oftentimes, it may take longer to reach your goal. Gradually, you will feel and see the difference. Others will eventually notice your gains. It is the same in the spiritual. As you continue to exert your faith, those muscles will grow. Your character will be chiseled as you continue your efforts to please Christ.

6. **Lock into your purpose.**

   I Corinthians 15:58 says, "Therefore, my beloved brethren, be ye stedfast, unmoveable, always abounding in the work of the Lord, forasmuch as ye know that your labour is not in vain in the Lord."

When you know who you are, you gain a level of strength you have never had. Knowing who you are means knowing what your purpose is. Individuals that know their purpose waste less time. They understand how valuable they are to the kingdom of God. They know they serve an intricate part. For this reason, they can stand firm. They are secure. They are confident. They are locked and loaded! You can be too.

PRAYER

Holy Spirit, I have not been operating to my full potential. My spiritual tank has been on low for some time. I have been operating in my own strength. Jesus, reset my thinking. Allow my actions to align with the change you have done within me. Help me to surround myself with others that can uplift me spiritually. Guide me into the path that pleases you. Engulf my thoughts. Season my tongue with your word. Help me to become more disciplined in my prayer life. I long to be in your presence. I know the more I practice this I will become stable. I do not want to be swayed in my faith. Thank you for your guidance and protection. Amen.

Chapter Four

UM, WHO ARE YOU TALKING TO?

The sound of the running water soothed her ears, knowing that the current shrills and thunderous footsteps would soon descend. She inhaled the smell of the lavender vanilla candle that drifted through the air while anticipating her desire for silence. It was the children's bath time, which would be followed by "mommy time." Although "mommy time" usually didn't last long, she was eager to engage in adult conversation or no conversation at all. Thoughts of hot water running down her back and embracing her achy feet intrigued her. She was excited to moisturize her skin with the lightly scented body lotion she purchased days ago. New business ventures were on her mind and she desired to share them with her husband. Suddenly he entered the bathroom and abruptly turned the faucet off. "They don't need that much water in the tub to wash," he stated.

Struggling to keep the words in her head from

leaping into the atmosphere and slapping him in the face, she bit her bottom lip instead. He said other things and his reasons were valid, but she believed his approach was less commendable. Her mood immediately shifted and her entire script changed. She wanted to ask, "Um, who are you talking to?" Her mind overflowed with so many words that it began to drown her desire for peace. Something in her now wanted to wage war. Determined not to subject herself to those feelings, she moved swiftly and silently to the other end of the house. It was best for her husband to finish the children's bath time. She prayed and asked God to close the mouth of her mind that wanted to get her husband straight. Her flesh sought to respond to his actions with fire.

Have you ever felt like you had the right to give a heated response in a situation? This wife was offended by her husband's actions. She felt insulted when he turned off the water as she sat in the bathroom. Surely, he knew that she was capable of running baths for the kids. Rather than politely mentioning his opinion regarding the bath water, he stepped in and turned it off. The wife immediately felt disrespected. After feeling burnt out and desiring to relax, she experiences a completely different emotion.

UM, WHO ARE YOU TALKING TO?

Admit it! You have asked someone this exact question, haven't you? You felt justified too, right? Now, analyze your response in that situation. **Did your physical response and the thoughts of your mind align?**

Proverbs 15:1 says, "A soft answer turneth away wrath: but grievous words stir up anger.

Neither the husband nor wife exemplified this scripture in their actions. Her husband's intentions were good and he meant no ill-will by his actions. The wife was responsible for how she chose to respond. Unfortunately, we cannot control the actions of others. We are only responsible for our actions. In this instance, the wife chose to remain vocally quiet. Her actions spoke differently though. It can be difficult to think and act with love and kindness when the same actions aren't reciprocated to you. However, the more you feed and practice God's word, it can become your natural response.

PRAYER

God, there are times when I am placed in a very uncomfortable position. I do not like being disrespected. In those times, I want to set people straight. I have failed in the past to keep my mouth shut. Honestly, I feel justified for saying some of the stuff I have said. There are times when I have kept quiet, but my mind has not. Your word declares that a soft answer can detour confusion. Help me not to relish in or gain excitement in chaos. When I am tested or tried, help me to respond and not react. While I am not there yet, I believe that one day I will be able to wish my enemies the best. Thank you in advance for the fulfillment of your word in me. Amen.

Chapter Five

WAS THAT SHADE?

As she entered the parking lot of her doctor's office, a young lady walked past her car. The warmth of the sun gleamed on her left arm through the driver's window. She glared at the female with perplexity. Because the woman's demeanor suggested she was lost, she assumed the same. It was almost noon and the temperature was a scorching 93 degrees. Grateful for the cool air blowing from her car vents onto her face, she dreaded exiting the car. Keeping her schedule in mind, she quickly entered the building.

The young lady sat alone in the lobby listening to her cell phone at a blaring volume. It was in her hand, just barely touching her long, wrinkled, khaki skirt. The ends were frayed and the material was rigid. Despite the intense heat, a black long-sleeved jacket and a white collared shirt accompanied her ensemble. Her clothes were tattered and her appearance was disheveled. Her hair looked overprocessed and full of split ends.

It was unclear if she was listening to a podcast or a sermon of some sort. The orator was a female, speaking on the dos and don'ts of godly women. The young lady audibly expressed her approval of the message with a few strong "um huhs" after each statement. The woman, who had observed the young lady while she sat in her car, now sat across from her. She was mentally engulfed in her to-do list. If she was going to be on time for Wednesday night service, her grocery shopping and cooking needed to be done quickly.

She peered at her nails, wondering when she would have time to visit the nail salon. It had been weeks since her last manicure and pedicure. At her last visit she opted not to stay in the pink family, per her norm. She chose the color "desert sun." It reminded her of a subtle tangerine hue. As she continued to wait to hear her name called by one of the nurses, the young woman continued to listened to her phone. The lecturer now spoke against nail polish. She specifically spoke against the color orange for being too bright. She continued to declare anyone wearing more than one color on their nails was attracting attention to themselves. Nail salons were deemed as a place of idol worship and declared the immaturity of those patrons.

The young lady turned the message off following

those comments. It could only be assumed that she noticed the woman sitting across from her in the lobby was indeed wearing orange nail polish. Never lifting her head up to acknowledge the young woman or the condemning message, she pondered upon the statements. She desperately wanted to question the young lady. There were so many misleading statements that she seemed to agree with. Shortly thereafter, the nurse called her name. Reluctantly, she left the lobby and proceeded with her appointment.

  As believers, we have been called to reach the lost. I am convinced that many members of the body of Christ have been unable to fulfill this task successfully due to an expected look. Not only are we failing to reach, but we are failing to be reached as well. The concept of how the person is supposed to look is misleading. Can God use someone with pink hair to deliver a message of truth? Absolutely. Can the individual with pink hair receive a message of truth from someone that looks nothing like them? Absolutely. Personal preferences can often be viewed as sin in the eyes of some. Many individuals have been pushed away from something because of their looks. Ironically, the woman wearing the "desert sun" nail polish was a seasoned, devout Christian. She was also a woman of faith. Her nail color choice did not speak of the condition of her heart.

 I remember visiting a women's conference and feeling slightly offended by a female pastor. The pastor's daughter was there with her. She was a sweet little girl that liked being around me. Her mom looked at me and commented, "Oh yea, she's really into all of that stuff." She extended her pointer finger and moved her hand up and down as she spoke. "I'm all natural," she said. Her tone was mixed with disapproval and mockery. I did not respond, but my mind definitely wondered about her comments. "Was that shade," I wondered. What was "all of that stuff" she was referring to? At the time, I was wearing my hair in a short cut with blonde highlights. Rather than its naturally curly state, it had been blown straight. I wore a nude pink lip gloss that was very close to my lip color. I did not wear any other makeup. There was nothing flashy about my casual black dress or shoes. I was specific in my attire, as not to offend the host church. However, I felt offended.

 I could not have received anything from her at that point, whether spiritual or natural. I felt like she looked at me and formed a negative opinion. The aforementioned scenario involving the woman wearing the orange nail polish was very similar. Both women were never given an opportunity to speak for themselves. I felt like the pastor's wife insulted me in an attempt to make herself look better. I could have been wrong. That type of behavior has never been admirable to me. It is hard for me to believe that it is honorable in the sight of God.

WAS THAT SHADE?

Let's be honest. Yes. The latter example included a direct insult given with a condescending undertone. The scenarios were different in nature, but both included a level of negative judgment about someone they didn't know. As followers of Christ, we are called to reach the lost. Those individuals may not look like us. They may have a different background. If we treat others with disdain prior to having a conversation with them, we will not reach the lost. Here are a few tips to assist you if you have been guilty of this behavior:

1. **Do not give random individuals the power to speak into your life.**
    Proverbs 13:20 says, "He that walketh with wise men shall be wise: But a companion of fools shall be destroyed."

Social media has created a platform for anyone with access to the internet to offer their opinion in order to gain a following. Oftentimes, their truths are not biblically based, but rather personal choices. Know the difference between the two. Do not waste time entertaining foolishness.

2. **Be careful how you place judgment on others.**

   John 7:24 says," Judge not according to the appearance, but judge righteous judgment."

In this particular verse of scripture, Jesus is being judged for healing a man on the sabbath day. Can you imagine how those people felt after being made aware of who he was. Nevertheless, he was seen in a negative light by others who deemed themselves righteous.

3. **Forgive others and yourself.**

   Romans 12:17-18 says, "Recompense to no man evil for evil. Provide things honest in the sight of all men. If it be possible, as much as lieth in you, live peaceably with all men.

When you have been mishandled by others, it is hard to forgive. However, it CAN be done. Choose to forgive those that you are holding in the jail cell of your mind. Now, free yourself. Choose to forgive yourself for how you have judged others. Most people avoid conversations about forgiveness. Sometimes it is not possible to discuss it with the individual centered around your pain. Not everyone is unavailable though. Talk about it, if you can. Push through! Ask and receive forgiveness.

PRAYER

Lord, forgive me for all the times I have passed unrighteous judgment on others. Help me to see and treat people with kindness and respect. Allow me to set a good example of your word through my actions. May the love that you have shown me extend to others. I want to draw them to you, not push them away. I choose to forgive others that have passed unrighteous judgment on me and treated me indifferently. I do not wish any evil on them. I will not dwell on my past mistakes or offenses. From this day forth, I will focus on the things that you have given me to do. Help me to fulfill the responsibilities you have given me. Amen.

Chapter Six

BUT WHY?

The sky was filled with beautiful hues of ginger and scarlet. Ribbons of gold furrowed throughout the various clouds as the sun began its departure. The cool crisp air tickled her ears reminding her that autumn had arrived. She opened the door for her toddler to exit the vehicle and grabbed his hand. "No running. Remember what Mommy told you about the parking lot," she said. She proceeded to explain to the child why they were going in the store. "We are not buying candy, ice cream or toys. I am only picking up a few things for dinner," she uttered. The toddler continued to skip and giggle without a care in the world.

Almost immediately upon entering the store, the pleading began. Determined to ignore the toddler's oos and aas, she focused on her list and made her way to the necessary items. They passed an elderly gentleman who chuckled at her child's persistent pleas for everything bright and shiny. She could hear cries coming from the next aisle over. Apparently, another mother was in the midst of a "no we are not buying that" war. She quickly grabbed her items and made her way to the register. She meticulously placed everything on the conveyor belt. Drinks were placed first, followed by rice and vegetables. The fruits were placed together. Soft and fragile items were also sectioned off.

The groceries were bagged accordingly and placed in the shopping cart. The mom noticed her son was being particularly quiet and still while waiting for her. She completed the transaction and loaded the groceries into the shopping cart. "Come on sweetheart," she said. They exited the door and proceeded to their car. After opening the door, her toddler hastily entered the car and closed the door. She continued to unload the groceries and then pushed the cart into the loading area next to the car.

She returned to the car, buckled her seatbelt, and turned on the engine. "Alright, we have groceries and we're all buckled up. Let's go home," she proclaimed. She peered through the rear-view mirror to check on the status of her child. She notices a lollipop. "Where did you get that from?" she shrieked.

"In the store," he answers with pride.

She is flooded with emotions as she grabs the lollipop from the child. "You can't take things just because you want them," she explains.

"But, why?" he asks.

"Son, taking things that don't belong to you is wrong. When we go to the store, we pay for the things we want. I told you before we went in that you were not going to get any candy. You hid this lollipop and then brought it out of the store. When we do things that are not right, we displease God.

She breathes hard, turns off the engine, unbuckles her seatbelt and exits the vehicle. Disappointed in his actions, she opens the back door and unbuckles the toddler.

"We're going back in Mommy?" he asks.

"Yes. We have to return this," she said. Embarrassed, she goes to the cashier and explains what happened.

"Oh, it's ok. I'm surprised you came back in for that," she said puzzled.

BUT WHY?

1. Integrity Matters

Proverbs 11:3 says, "The integrity of the upright shall guide them: but the perverseness of transgressors shall destroy them."

The morals of society are at an all-time low. They are

continually decreasing. Genuine goodness in mankind is depleting. Some individuals will justify not returning the lollipop because it is not costly and no store employees were aware of the situation. However, it is not about the cost of the lollipop. It is about the character of the individual.

2. Your children are watching.

Proverbs 22:6 says, "Train up a child in the way he should go: and when he is old, he will not depart from it."

The choices parents display before their children are often duplicated by those same children later in life. Simple choices lead to bigger choices. In the above scenario the mother could have easily chosen to allow her son to just eat the stolen lollipop. After all, it wasn't a costly item and nobody saw him take it. However, the chances of him continuing to make the same decision later on are greater. He may also feel justified.

PRAYER

Father, help me to please you even when no one is looking. I want to make wise decisions and be a great example for others. Forgive me for my displeasing ways. My character matters. I am an extension of you. My fraudulent ways have misled others and displayed my lack of integrity. I will no longer justify my wrongdoings in an attempt to conceal the deception of my mind. I take responsibility for my dishonest thoughts. As *Psalms 51:10 says, "Create in me a clean heart, O God; and renew a right spirit within me."* Thank you for performing this work in me. Amen.

Chapter Seven

WHO TOLD YOU THAT?

She took one last look at herself in the mirror before exiting the door. While double checking her bag, she did a quick look through to ensure nothing was missing. "Ok, I've got my keys, phone, lipstick, mascara, resume and cover letter. I'm all set," she thought. She began rehearsing her strengths and weaknesses speech to herself. Confident of her skills and knowledge of the profession, she felt ready.

Upon arriving for her interview, she noticed the small number of windows in the building. "Hmm, not much sunlight," she pondered. Slight dizziness and labored breathing began to take over her body. Her nerves were getting the best of her. "Breathe, just breathe," she whispered to herself. She opened the door and stood next to her car as she prayed silently. Slowly, she turned and faced the building. With a determined mind, she proceeded inside.

If you've ever been to a job interview, you know the level of stress involved. Self-doubt can set in before you enter the facility. The idea of proving yourself worthy to strangers can be overwhelming. I have been to interviews where there was a panel of interviewers. Each of them was there to ask a different set of questions and sum you up in their own way.

  I remember interviewing for a job very similar to a position that I excelled in for a number of years. I was eager to get this job because it offered better pay, better benefits and was located in the city I desired to work in. When I did not get the position, I was devastated. I replayed that interview in my head over and over. I reviewed my cover letter and resume numerous times. I even spoke to my references. At one point, I was tempted to call the job and inquire their reason for not accepting me.

  Without realizing, I began to discredit myself. One day I asked God to give me peace of mind. Then, I thought about my feelings. My self-evaluation was enlightening. Unlike other people I knew, denial of job positions hurt me deeply. My pain centered around the feelings of not being good enough. I heard God ask, "Who told you that?" Memories began to flood my mind.

  I had suppressed certain feelings over time. These feelings formed when I was younger. I remember hearing people compare me to others. I questioned my complexion.

Perhaps, my skin was too dark. I questioned my size. Maybe, my body was too big. I questioned my hair, wondering if it was too thick or not long enough. None of these memories came from my immediate family members or people that I considered influential. Somehow, the words that were said bothered me subconsciously. My view of "good enough" started equating to a certain look which eventually included the matching job. I was attempting to meet man-made standards, not God's. Let's evaluate some of the deceptions that you may have embraced.

WHO TOLD YOU THAT?

YOU SAY:	GOD SAYS:
I am sick.	You are healed. Jeremiah 17:14
I am afraid.	Fear not. II Timothy 1:7
I am not worthy.	Everyone has fallen. Romans 3:23
I am weak.	Rely on my strength. II Corinthians 12:9

I don't look the part.	I specialize in using the underdog. I used David to defeat a giant twice his size. I Samuel 17
I don't sound right.	There is nothing wrong with your voice. Moses thought this too. I used him to lead the Israelites out of bondage. Exodus 7-13
I'm not good enough.	Yes, you are. I live within you. I Corinthians 3:16
I am angry.	Ok, don't sin though. Get it together tonight. Ephesians 4:26-27

There is no need to rely on your physical, mental or emotional capabilities. Stop listening to the lies that hold you back from greatness. You can have more. You can be more because there is more for you to do. Sis, get up! Get up out of your bed of affliction. Wave goodbye to despair. Close the door to fear. Pack up the baggage of self-condemnation. It is no longer welcome in your heart. Disassociate yourself from those inherited, consented, and unconsented strongholds you have entertained. Rebuke them from the lives of your children (even if they don't exist yet). Serve notice on the enemy that those tactics no longer work and give him his eviction notice. Stand firm in your convictions. Declare prosperity over you and yours. Embrace hope. YOU HAVE WORK TO DO!

PRAYER

Lord, I want to be who you have called me to be. Refuel every area of my life that I lack strength, ability or motivation. Help me to accomplish the work you have for me. I lay aside pride, doubt, fear and the pain of my past. I choose to intentionally move forward and not return to any of the ways that have displeased you. Forgive me for losing sight of my purpose at times. From this day forth, I declare and decree that I will accomplish the work you have for me to do. Amen!

NOTES

Notes

Acknowledgments

To Shone:

I am blessed to share life with you. Thank you for the push that you continue to provide. Your words of encouragement have not fallen on deaf ears. I am appreciative of your unconditional love and support.

To Micaiah and Zion:

God knew I needed you. I will continue to make every effort to be the best mommy for you both. I believe you are destined for greatness. May my life serve as a map to thrust you into the path of greatness that lies within you.

Made in the USA
Columbia, SC
10 December 2023